A Hide-and-Seek Book

Mother Goose Rhymes

by Katy Keck Arnsteen

DERRYDALE BOOKS
New York

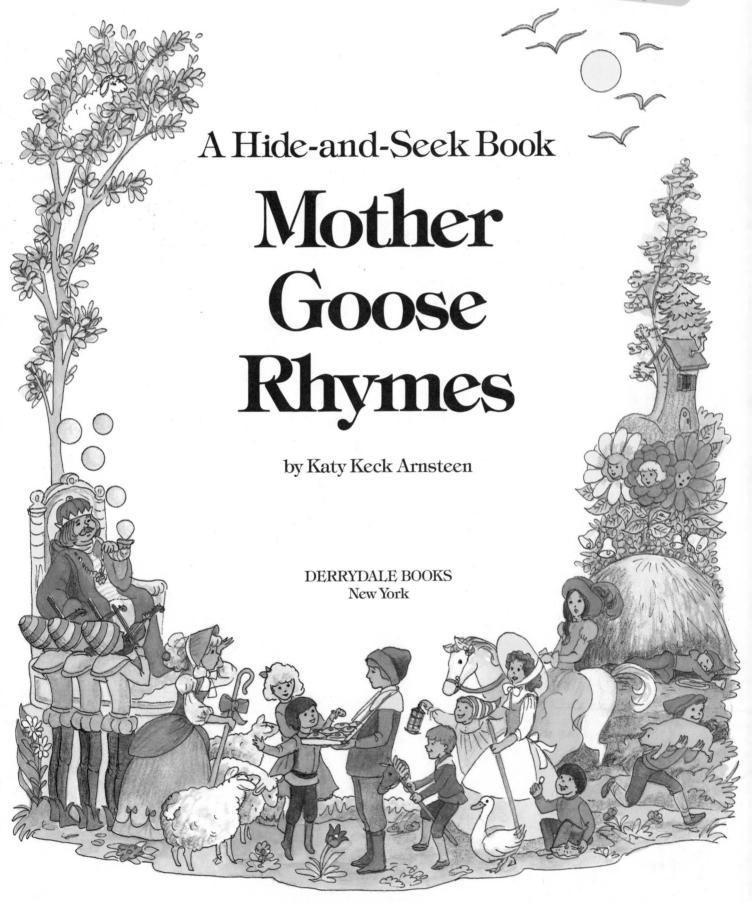

Simple Simon

The pieman lost five of his pies at the fair. Can you find them?

Little Jack Horner

Little Jack Horner has lost a slice of his Christmas pie. Can you help him find it?

Mary, Mary, Quite Contrary

Mary, Mary, quite contrary, gave away five silver bells from her garden. Can you find all five?

Wee Willie Winkie

Wee Willie Winkie is ready for bed, but he can't find his lantern to light the way home. Do you know where it is?

Old King Cole

Old King Cole called for his pipe and his bowl and his fiddlers three, but one fiddler is missing. Where can he be?

Little Bo Peep

Little Bo Peep has lost six of her
sheep and doesn't know where to
find them. Can you help her?

Sing a Song of Sixpence

Four and twenty blackbirds were baked in the king's pie, and so was one bluebird. Where is the bluebird?

Little Boy Blue

Little Boy Blue has lost his horn.
Can you help him find it?

The Old Woman
Who Lived in a Shoe

The Old Woman sent her children to bed without any bread. Can you find the loaf of bread?